A Closer Look at
ANCIENT EGYPT

A CLOSER LOOK BOOK
ⓒ The Archon Press Ltd
1977

Designed by David Cook and
Associates and produced by
The Archon Press Ltd
8 Butter Market
Ipswich IP1 1BN

The author wishes to
acknowledge the assistance
received from
W. V. Davies
Assistant Keeper of Egyptology
The British Museum, London
during the preparation
of this book

0 906290 47 3

First published in
Great Britain by
Hamish Hamilton
Children's Books Ltd

New Scimitar Edition 1981
Printed in Great Britain by
W. S. Cowell Ltd
Butter Market, Ipswich

A closer LOOK at ANCIENT EGYPT

Wendy Boase

Illustrated by
Angus McBride, Eric Thomas

Scimitar · Ipswich

The kingdom of Egypt

Face of the God-Kings
Despite the magnificence of their surviving buildings, many of Egypt's rulers remain for us, shadowy figures. Reading their portraits from top to bottom we encounter: Zoser of the Old Kingdom, Cheops, builder of the Great Pyramid, and Amenmhet III. Then Queen Hatshepsut, her warrior stepson Tuthmosis III, and Ramesses II who reigned for 67 years; all dynamic rulers of the New Kingdom.

As it runs through the barren North African desert, the River Nile creates around itself a narrow strip of rich and fertile land – the country of Egypt. This long, narrow land, protected by rocky desert on either side, with its great river providing a highway for trade and administration from one end to the other, was the setting for one of the most enduring civilisations of the ancient world – one which lasted over 3,000 years.

The first people to live in the fertile Nile valley were prehistoric hunters, driven north from the drought-parched grasslands of central Africa. These tribesmen settled along the banks of the Nile, establishing small farming communities, and worshipping the animal totems they had brought with them. (Later, these developed into the many local gods of Ancient Egypt.) Eventually, two distinct kingdoms emerged – Upper (southern) and Lower (northern) Egypt.

Traditionally, the two kingdoms were united by King Narmer (also called Menes), ruler of Upper Egypt. An ancient stone palette has survived showing how Narmer triumphed over the people of the north. He is wearing the crown of Lower Egypt and has ten headless bodies (presumably northerners) lying at his feet.

The history of Egypt can be divided into a number of distinct periods – within which the dynasties, or ruling families, of kings can be grouped. Narmer was the first pharaoh of the Ist dynasty.

A time of great prosperity for the country began with the rule of the IVth dynasty – the period called the Old Kingdom. This saw the building of the first great monuments to Egyptian power and skill: the pyramids, tombs of the pharaohs.

The last pharaohs of the Old Kingdom were weak and power slipped from their grasp. The result was over 200 years of chaos, known as the First Intermediate period. The princes of Thebes emerged as rulers of the country after the civil war.

From their capital at Thebes, the Middle Kingdom pharaohs of the XIth and XIIth dynasties sent out trading and military expeditions, extending the southern borders of the country. But a time of peace and prosperity was destroyed once more by a series of obscure and apparently ineffectual pharaohs in the XIIIth and XIVth dynasties. The Second Intermediate period was one of the darkest in Egypt's history. The country was invaded and overrun by war-like nomads from the east, armed with horses and chariots. These people, the Hyksos, or 'Shepherd Kings', overwhelmed the disorganised Egyptians and seized the country for over 300 years.

Once again the rulers of Thebes asserted themselves and drove out the invaders – after learning to use their enemies' weapons. The 400-year-span of the New Kingdom which followed was the most splendid epoch in Egyptian history. But the splendour and glory faded. During the Late Dynastic period the country was ruled by a succession of foreigners. With the death of Cleopatra, last of the Greek Ptolemies, the Egyptian empire became a mere province of Rome.

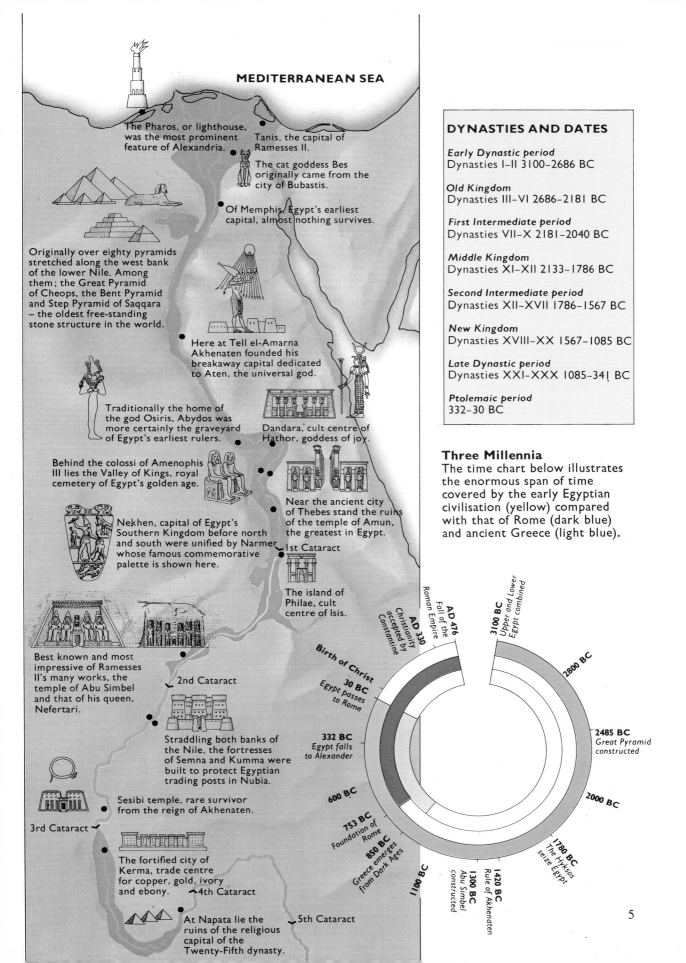

MEDITERRANEAN SEA

The Pharos, or lighthouse, was the most prominent feature of Alexandria.

Tanis, the capital of Ramesses II.

The cat goddess Bes originally came from the city of Bubastis.

Of Memphis, Egypt's earliest capital, almost nothing survives.

Originally over eighty pyramids stretched along the west bank of the lower Nile. Among them; the Great Pyramid of Cheops, the Bent Pyramid and Step Pyramid of Saqqara – the oldest free-standing stone structure in the world.

Here at Tell el-Amarna Akhenaten founded his breakaway capital dedicated to Aten, the universal god.

Traditionally the home of the god Osiris, Abydos was more certainly the graveyard of Egypt's earliest rulers.

Dandara, cult centre of Hathor, goddess of joy.

Behind the colossi of Amenophis III lies the Valley of Kings, royal cemetery of Egypt's golden age.

Near the ancient city of Thebes stand the ruins of the temple of Amun, the greatest in Egypt.

Nekhen, capital of Egypt's Southern Kingdom before north and south were unified by Narmer whose famous commemorative palette is shown here.

1st Cataract

The island of Philae, cult centre of Isis.

Best known and most impressive of Ramesses II's many works, the temple of Abu Simbel and that of his queen, Nefertari.

2nd Cataract

Straddling both banks of the Nile, the fortresses of Semna and Kumma were built to protect Egyptian trading posts in Nubia.

Sesibi temple, rare survivor from the reign of Akhenaten.

3rd Cataract

The fortified city of Kerma, trade centre for copper, gold, ivory and ebony.

4th Cataract

At Napata lie the ruins of the religious capital of the Twenty-Fifth dynasty.

5th Cataract

DYNASTIES AND DATES

Early Dynastic period
Dynasties I–II 3100–2686 BC

Old Kingdom
Dynasties III–VI 2686–2181 BC

First Intermediate period
Dynasties VII–X 2181–2040 BC

Middle Kingdom
Dynasties XI–XII 2133–1786 BC

Second Intermediate period
Dynasties XII–XVII 1786–1567 BC

New Kingdom
Dynasties XVIII–XX 1567–1085 BC

Late Dynastic period
Dynasties XXI–XXX 1085–341 BC

Ptolemaic period
332–30 BC

Three Millennia

The time chart below illustrates the enormous span of time covered by the early Egyptian civilisation (yellow) compared with that of Rome (dark blue) and ancient Greece (light blue).

AD 476 Fall of the Roman Empire

AD 330 Christianity accepted by Constantine

Birth of Christ

30 BC Egypt passes to Rome

332 BC Egypt falls to Alexander

600 BC

753 BC Foundation of Rome

850 BC Greece emerges from Dark Ages

1100 BC

1300 BC Abu Simbel constructed

1420 BC Rule of Akhenaten

1780 BC The Hyksos seize Egypt

2000 BC

2485 BC Great Pyramid constructed

2800 BC

3100 BC Upper and Lower Egypt combined

Forging an empire

Symbols of royal power
In early times each province of Egypt depicted its god as an animal and used it as an emblem, or totem. The white crown of Upper Egypt carried a cobra's head while the red crown of Lower Egypt originally bore a vulture. When the two kingdoms were united the pharaohs of the Two Lands wore both animals on a red and white double crown.

To the Egyptians, the pharaoh was the representative on earth of the sun god, Amun, and all the land and people of Egypt belonged to him. Elaborate ceremonial reinforced the impression of his god-like power.

Some of the greatest pharaohs in Egyptian history ruled during the period of the New Kingdom. Tuthmosis I, of the XVIIIth dynasty, fought a campaign in Nubia and extended the southern frontier as far as the third cataract on the Nile. 'His Majesty sailed downstream,' reported one of his commanders, 'with all countries in his grasp and all that miserable Nubian chief hanged head downward at the prow of the barge of His Majesty.'

Another outstanding pharaoh of the XVIIIth dynasty was a woman, Queen Hatshetsup, widow of Tuthmosis II, and stepmother of Tuthmosis III. Like the male pharaohs, she claimed divine birth and statues show her wearing the double crown and even the ceremonial royal beard! The queen is remembered for her beautiful temple at Deir el-Bahri.

After Hatshetsup's death, her stepson obliterated her name and image from buildings and monuments. Then, for almost every spring of his reign, he mounted military expeditions to Asia, subduing rebellious lands and exacting tribute from their kings. With this treasure, he built magnificent halls and gateways to Amun, god of Thebes, at Karnak. Because of his conquests and his short stature, Tuthmosis has been called the Napoleon of Egypt.

Perhaps the best known pharaoh of the next, the XIXth dynasty, is Ramesses II, 'the Great'. His long reign (over 60 years) began with almost 20 years of continuous warfare against the Hittites. After a decisive battle at Kadish, in Syria, peace was established and Ramesses devoted the rest of his reign to vast building projects like the mighty temple at Abu Simbel.

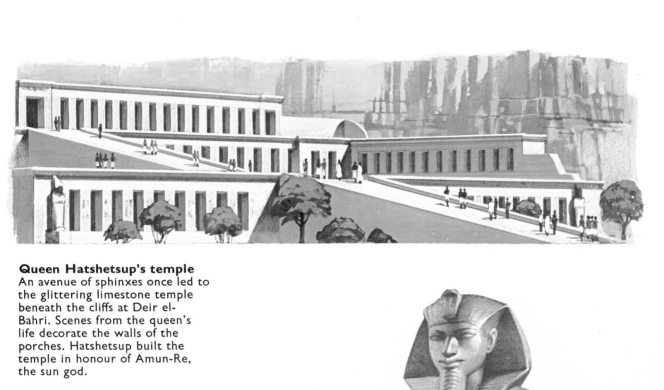

Queen Hatshetsup's temple

An avenue of sphinxes once led to the glittering limestone temple beneath the cliffs at Deir el-Bahri. Scenes from the queen's life decorate the walls of the porches. Hatshetsup built the temple in honour of Amun-Re, the sun god.

Moving a colossus

Giant statues, or colossi, of the New Kingdom pharaohs, emphasised their power and reflected their personal arrogance. About 172 sturdy labourers were needed to move a 60-tonne statue, using sledges, levers and ropes.

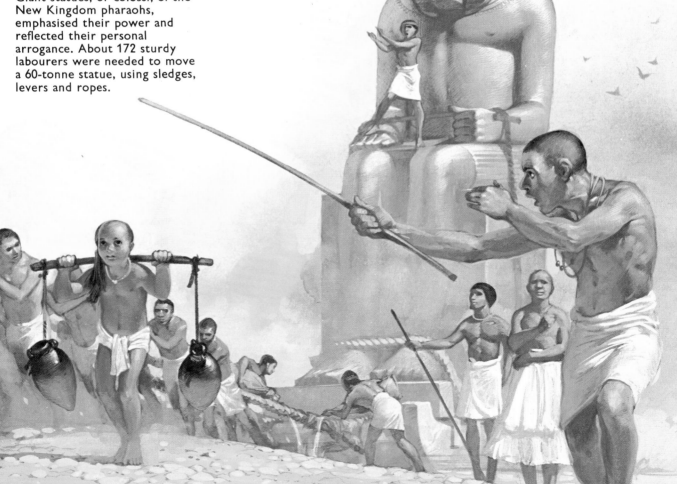

The land of Egypt

The rich and splendid civilisation of Ancient Egypt was based on a prosperous farming economy. From the rugged country of Upper Egypt (in the south) to the gentler Delta (in the north), the land blossomed. Crops of wheat and barley, fruit and vegetables, and herd animals were all nourished by the rich black soil, watered by the Nile. The colour of the soil led the Egyptians to call their country *Kemet*, 'the black land'.

The life of the Egyptian peasants who laboured on the land was hard – but they knew that their hard work almost always brought a just reward. The farming year was divided into three predictable seasons, which depended on the behaviour of the Nile. The 'inundation' (or flooding) lasted from June until September; then the Nile overflowed its banks and flooded the fields. When the water went down it left the fields covered with a layer of rich silt which lasted until February. During this period, the peasants sowed their crops and dug the vitally important irrigation ditches. In the 'drought' that followed, from March to May, they harvested the crops. As well as cultivated crops, the Egyptians harvested the naturally-growing papyrus reed, from which they made paper, boats, baskets, mats, ropes and sandals. When the flood returned the peasants laboured on the pharaoh's great building projects. Huge stone blocks could be floated on rafts on the flood water.

Of course, there were bad years, when the regular cycle of flood and drought was broken and the crops failed. But food could be stored against a bad year – as Joseph advised the pharaoh in the Bible story to do during the 'seven lean years' he foresaw in his dream – and good irrigation systems helped too.

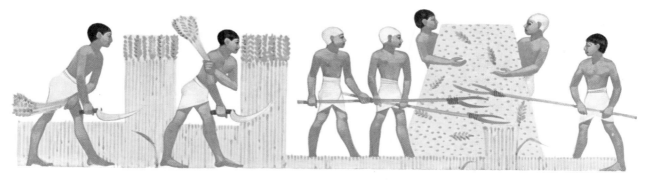

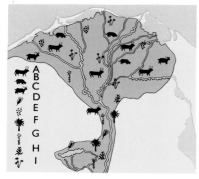

The fertile Delta

At the end of its 4,000-mile journey the ancient Nile emptied itself into the Mediterranean in seven separate waterways, making Lower Egypt the most fertile area in the country. Landowners raised fat cattle (A), pigs (B) and goats (C) here. Barley (D), grapes (E) and date palms (F) were grown, flax (G) for weaving linen and the sesame plant (H) for its oil-bearing seeds. Papyrus (I) grew in wild profusion and the waterfowl which lived in the marshes — cranes, geese and ducks — made excellent eating.

The farmer's year

This frieze, like those which decorate the temples and tombs of Egypt, shows the busy life of an agricultural people.

In preparation for planting, the ground is broken up by hand or with wooden ploughs drawn by cattle. Grain is sown in the rich Nile soil. The harvest is cut with flint-toothed sickles and stacked with wooden forks. Donkeys were used as beasts of burden, but here they thresh grain by walking over it. Papyrus reeds are gathered and the geese, which live among them, are driven home to be fattened. Honey is collected, as sugar was unknown to the Egyptians. Grapes are picked and pressed for their juice. Long-horned cattle, which were also slaughtered for meat, are being milked here. Farming is helped by the shaduf, a bucket on a pole used to fill the ditches which irrigate the drier land. By a guiding rope, the bucket is lowered into the Nile; a heavy counterweight on the other end of the pole raises it again, brimming with valuable water.

9

The craft of war

Prisoners of war
Foreign captives were bound and branded as slaves. They included Libyans, Nubians, the Hittites, Syrians and Mitanni of Asia, Semites from Palestine and, later, the Sea Peoples from across the Mediterranean.

Although its history contains some notable battles, the civilisation of Ancient Egypt was not essentially a military one based on conquest by force of arms. Scenes of battles painted and carved on tombs of the Old Kingdom show that the Egyptians had soldiers and knew something of warfare and armour. But at that time they did not have a national army as such. In an emergency, the provincial governors, like the barons of medieval Europe, could call up an impressive feudal army from among the peasants. The foot soldiers fought almost naked with bronze- and copper-tipped spears, small axes and bows.

When the pharaohs of the Middle Kingdom restored order after a period of chaos and civil war, they abolished the system of local levies – which local leaders could use to fight against each other – and set up a trained, central army under the command of the king.

Although the new Egyptian army was disciplined and reasonably well equipped, it was no match for the Hyksos when they swept into the Nile valley in their horse-drawn chariots, in 1786 BC. These Asiatic warrior kings, armed with bronze swords and powerful bows, controlled the country for 200 years until the Egyptians, having learnt to use both the chariots and the weapons of their enemies, drove the foreigners out.

United again under the New Kingdom rulers, Egypt made her own plans for conquest against Near and Middle East neighbours

The war machine
The chariots that sped the pharaohs into battle were light and strong. They could wheel and turn easily in a tight space.

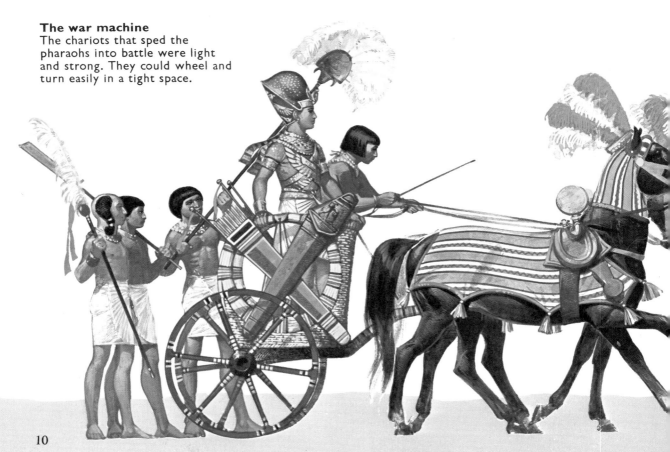

who were growing stronger and more menacing. The pharaoh himself led his army into battle, sometimes accompanied by a trained lion. Now the professional soldiers were equipped with body armour and the latest weapons. Archers were provided with bronze-tipped arrows and strong bows made of wood, animal sinew and horn. Other soldiers wielded spears with metal tips, axes, bronze daggers and scimitars – the wickedly curved swords borrowed from the Syrians. The infantry was supported by chariots. Manned by a driver and an archer, the chariots raced across the enemy front, firing into their ranks.

In the New Kingdom period, Egyptian troops won a famous victory at sea. Ramesses III met the Mediterranean fleet raised by the Sea Peoples in 1190 BC with a solid wall of Egyptian warships. Armed only with swords and spears and out-manoeuvred by the Egyptian oarsmen, the enemy vessels capsized under a storm of arrows fired from the decks of Ramesses' ships.

Although the tentacles of the Egyptian empire stretched over a vast area, her grip was strongest on her southern neighbour, Nubia. An Egyptian viceroy ruled here and a chain of forts, 160 kilometres long, guarded the road to the rich Nubian gold mines and protected Egypt from the warlike people of Kush, further south. In the New Kingdom these forts were partly garrisoned with colonial troops.

An infantry review
Middle Kingdom foot-soldiers were armed with bows and arrows, spears, slings and axes. For defence they relied on shields made of bulls' hide.

Frontier strongholds
Egyptian forts had thick walls and massive towers of masonry and mud-brick. Strong gates and a wide dry ditch protected them from attack. The forts were garrisoned by conscripted soldiers, and strengthened with professional shock-troops.

11

Shipping and trade

Papyrus boat
This was made of bundles of papyrus reed lashed together.

Trading with the land of Punt
Queen Hatshetsup sent a trading expedition to the land of Punt important enough to be recorded in detail in pictures on the walls of her temple at Deir el-Bahri. Five galleys travelled to Punt carrying necklaces, daggers and hatchets. The Egyptians are shown being greeted by the king and queen of the country. Hatshetsup's ships returned laden with wood, ivory, incense and incense trees, animal skins and even a live panther. Trading vessels like the one below were fitted with special tackle for loading heavy cargo such as timber.

The world's oldest picture of a boat comes from Egypt. Living on the banks of the great River Nile, the Egyptians depended on water transport above all else. Prehistoric Egyptians paddled down the river on papyrus rafts. As early as 3000 years BC, they were building wooden ships with sails. Oarsmen could be used on the river, but in the network of narrow canals men had to pull their boats along towpaths with ropes.

At the height of the Egyptian empire the Nile was like the bustling thoroughfare of a great city: flimsy reed boats and tiny ferries jostled among huge freighters loaded with grain or cattle, 70-metre-long barges bearing massive obelisks, and the slender galleys of government officials. Magnificent vessels carried the sacred images of the gods on the river at festivals.

The Egyptians ventured on to the open sea, too, at an early date. During the Old Kingdom, the pharaoh Sahure sent eight armed ships across the Mediterranean to attack the Syrian coasts. Another ruler, Seneferu, established an important trading link when he sent forty ships to the Lebanon to buy cedar for shipbuilding.

In the New Kingdom, when Egyptian power and wealth was at its peak, both land and sea trading routes were in constant use. As there was no 'money' (coins were not used until the 4th century BC), Egypt bartered linen, papyrus and other materials for foreign goods. The Egyptians took gold from Nubia and traded it for African ebony, ivory and animal skins. Caravans of donkeys wound east in to the Sinai desert to the turquoise and copper mines. Galleys sailed down the Red Sea to Punt, the land of perfume, gums and resin. Horses, cattle, silver, bronze and rare woods were shipped from Asia, as well as finished products such as chariots from Syria and jewellery from Babylon, to satisfy the Egyptians' exotic tastes.

From the river to the sea
At the bottom of the picture is a
Nile sailing craft of 3000 BC;
above it are: Sahure's sea-going
ship (2500 BC), Hatshetsup's
galley (1500 BC), and Ramesses
III's warship (1200 BC).

Ramesses III's war galley
1200 BC

Hatshepsut's trading galley
1500 BC

Sahure's sea-going vessel
2500 BC

Nile sailing craft
3000 BC

13

Society and the law

Egyptian society was organised in a way that changed remarkably little in over 3000 years. The Egyptians believed that the gods had created the world according to a ruling principle of truth and justice, called *maet*. Since they felt that everything, including the social system, was just as the gods wanted it to be, the Egyptians were not a people who liked change. The art of Ancient Egypt reflects this conservatism. The figures portrayed on the first King, Narmer's, stone palette are in the same, essentially unchanging style as those that decorate the tombs in the Valley of the Kings.

Society was headed by the pharaoh. He was the personification of the quality of *maet*. In early times the pharaoh alone was the head of the administration in name and deed. As civilisation advanced and the kingdom became richer and more powerful, governing it became more complicated. From the Middle Kingdom time, the pharaohs began to appoint officials to help them carry out their duties. Many of these were scribes or clerks in government offices, for there was a vast amount of writing to do – especially in connection with taxation, which was collected in kind (in actual goods, like corn or animals). By the time of the New Kingdom, the pharaoh had one chief minister, called a vizier, who oversaw national agriculture and held a high court of justice.

The vizier and the other chief officials, with the priests and nobles, formed the upper class of society. Beneath them, were scribes, soldiers, craftsmen, cattle herders, labourers, slaves and a mass of peasants. The children of peasants usually remained peasants, the sons of craftsmen were trained to be craftsmen, and noblemen's sons inherited their fathers' position. Literacy was the key to advancement but some distinguished soldiers could rise to higher ranks.

In spite of its rigid structure, Egyptian society had a humane and personal element in it. This is shown in the way women and slaves were treated – for, unusually in the civilisations of the ancient world, both had legal rights.

The divine Maet
World order, truth and justice were represented in the goddess, Maet, whose symbol was an ostrich feather. To the pharaohs, living by *maet* meant ruling justly; to the peasants it meant working honestly.

A court of law
Village chiefs, accused of not collecting taxes properly, are brought to trial. The vizier, the highest official under the pharaoh, presides over the court and acts as judge. The scribes record everything that happens. Sometimes special scribes helped defendants to prepare their cases. The vizier announced his verdict after he had read written evidence and heard what the witnesses had to say. A guilty man could be imprisoned or flogged. The contemporary frieze (**bottom left**) shows penitents kneeling before the court to beg for mercy.

The gods

The many curious-looking gods worshipped in Ancient Egypt, with their human bodies and animal heads, look strange, even frightening to us today. To the Egyptians, however, they were a comforting and familiar part of daily life. The earliest gods, like those of most prehistoric peoples, were associated with natural forces beyond man's control – the sun, the wind, the rise and fall of the Nile. Many of them reflected animal qualities that were particularly feared or admired – the fierceness of a lion or the strength of a bull – and, at first, all the gods had animal forms.

Before the kingdom of Egypt was united under the first pharaohs, it consisted of numerous tribal settlements, with their own totems, which gradually developed into local gods. Sometimes the influence of one god spread beyond its own little centre. This happened with Amun, god of Thebes, who was originally represented as a ram or a goose. He grew in importance with the rise of Thebes as the capital city. By the time of the New Kingdom, Amun was recognised as the king of the gods and great temples were raised in his honour at Karnak on the opposite bank of the Nile. All that remained of his animal origins were the two feathers worn at the back of the god's head in his statues.

Amun was also incorporated into the myths and stories connected with Re, the sun god – his name was combined with Re's and they were worshipped as one god, Amun-Re. Later gods, Osiris, lord of the underworld, and his wife/sister Isis, the great mother goddess, were brought into the 'family' of the older gods in the same way.

Neith of Sais

Ptah of Memphis

Re

Anubis

Sebek

Horus of Edfu

Shu

Isis

Ua of

Horus the child

Amun of Thebes

The creation of the world

Egyptians pictured the sky as a star-spangled goddess called Nut and the earth as her husband-brother, Geb. Before the creation of the universe Geb and Nut lived together. But Re, the sun-god who emerged from the waters of chaos, ordered them to be separated. Their father, Shu, created space and light between them by causing a great wind to lift Nut's body into the air. Shu became god of atmosphere. Geb lies below, forming the mountains and valleys of the earth. During the day, Re travelled across the arc formed by Nut's body. At night the sky goddess descended to her husband, thus creating darkness. Geb and Nut were the parents of Osiris, Isis and Set. Osiris was murdered by his jealous brother, Set, but Isis, his sister-wife, embalmed his body and thus gave Osiris the power to live again. The Egyptians believed that by preserving the body they, too, could live after death.

Mut

Thoth

Mestert

Osiris

Sekhmet

e of Thoth

Khnum

Nephthys

Khonsu

Sons of Horus

Hathor

Temples and priests

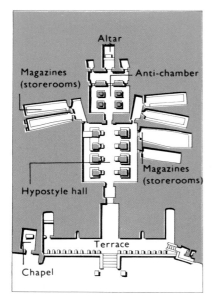

Abu Simbel
This mighty temple, cut out of the living rock, was dedicated by its builder, Ramesses II, to the sun god, Re. Its position and interior structure (above) were designed for the worship of the sun at dawn. A row of baboons, sacred to Thoth, god of wisdom, and the rising sun, ornament the frieze of the pharaoh's mortuary temple. The four statues of the pharaoh (right), once painted in glowing colours, are 20 metres high.

Egyptian temples were built to honour the gods and to record the deeds of the pharaohs, who hoped to join them after death. Every ruler regarded it as his duty to erect a temple or to add shrines, courtyards, gateways and statues to those built by earlier pharaohs. As certain gods grew in importance, the priests who served in their temples and interpreted their wishes became increasingly powerful.

During the New Kingdom, the mightiest divinity was Amun, the patron god of Thebes. At Karnak, near Thebes, the greatest temple ever built was dedicated to him and he owned more slaves, cattle, land and gold than any other god. Generations of pharaohs added to the Karnak temple, which grew from a small XIIth dynasty shrine into a complex large enough to hold a dozen European cathedrals. Its most impressive feature was the work of Ramesses II, the most ambitious builder of all the pharaohs. He erected the massive Hypostyle Hall (its name comes from the Greek, meaning 'to rest on pillars'). Its roof is supported by 134 columns, each one carved with scenes showing the pharaoh worshipping Amun.

At Abu Simbel, 480 kilometres south of Thebes, Ramesses built two more temples. The inner sanctuary of the larger, cut 55 metres into the living rock, is reached by the rays of the sun on only two days in each year – 23rd February and 23rd October. For the rest of the time the huge statues of Ramesses and the gods in the interior are shrouded in cold darkness. So, too, are the carvings on the ceilings, walls and pillars, which show the king – always twice his normal size – smiting his enemies.

Although the temples were vast, they formed part of an even larger complex which included houses for the priests, a school, storerooms and workshops. Priests had many duties. Some performed daily rituals in the funerary temples of the dead pharaohs. Others spent one month in four serving the gods in their special temples all over the country. Only a few chosen priests were allowed to enter the temple itself. Each day they approached the inner shrine in which a statue of the god was kept. The High Priest broke the clay seal on the doors and, chanting prayers, bowed down before the image. The god was taken out and bathed, clothed in fresh garments and anointed with oils. The statue was then resealed in its sanctuary with its offering of food and drink.

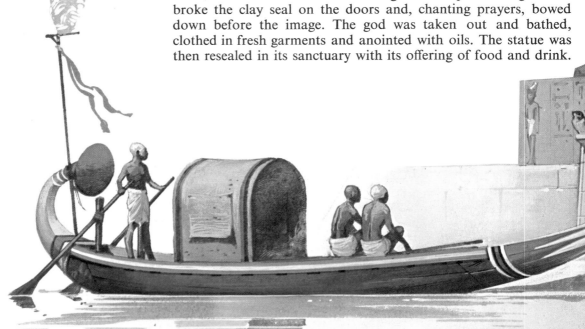

A revolutionary pharaoh

In the 14th century BC the power of the priests and traditional religion was challenged by the strangest pharaoh of all. Amenophis IV startled his people by introducing a new religion based upon worship of a single god. His reign saw a new name given to the pharaoh, the founding of a new capital city and the forging of a revolutionary art style. To the conservative Egyptians it must have seemed that their world was being turned upside down.

For almost 2000 years Egypt had prayed to a bewildering variety of gods. Monotheism, or the worship of one god, had never existed. We do not know what led the pharaoh to his belief, but he chose the Aten to be honoured above all gods. The Aten was the sun's disk, or the visible part of the sun which sends its warm beams down to earth.

Amenophis worshipped the Aten so fervently that he changed his name to Akhenaten ('He who serves the Aten'). His queen, the beautiful Nefertiti, added to her name, Nefer-neferu-Aten ('Fair is the goodness of the Aten'). The pharaoh began to build temples to Aten at Thebes. All the other gods, including Amun himself, special god of the capital city, were neglected.

Amun, however, was a mighty god and Akhenaten must have felt uncomfortable in his city. The pharaoh built a new capital, Akhet-Aten, 200 kilometres north of Thebes. In the arid desert, lakes, gardens and painted pavements appeared among royal temples and the mansions of high officials. An immense palace, 770 metres long, faced the Nile. Everywhere temples and tombs were decorated with scenes of everyday life and portraits of people, even of the pharaoh, in realistic poses.

Although minor figures like dancers and dwarves had been painted in a natural manner before, the pharaoh and his family

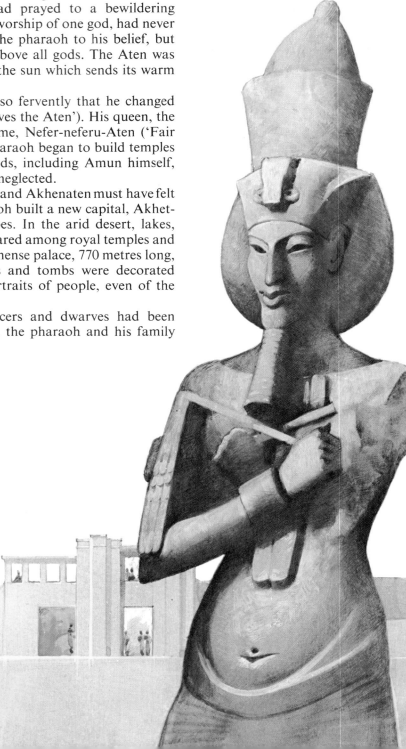

The sun's disk
Aten had existed as a form of the sun god from early times. It represented the sun at its zenith and was shown as a red disk with rays descending to the earth. Akhenaten made it the supreme god and altered its old image. He encircled the disk symbol with a *uraeus*, or rearing serpent – the ancient sign of royal power – to indicate the Aten's regal position.

had always appeared in formal, traditional scenes. The domestic life of Akhenaten's palace was shown – Nefertiti with a daughter on her knee, Akhenaten and his queen holding hands, two of their daughters lolling on cushions. The appearance of Akhenaten himself is disturbing: a distorted skull, drooping shoulders, pot belly and fat thighs characterise his portraits. Because this naturalistic art form flourished at Akhet-Aten, the modern Tell el-Amarna, it is known as the Amarna style.

But the Amarna period was only a brief flicker in the long history of Egyptian civilisation. When Akhenaten died, his successor, Tutankhamun, returned to Thebes and reinstated the old religion – and the old art.

The beautiful Nefertiti

Judging from royal portrait groups found in the ruins, Nefertiti, loving mother and devoted wife, must have spent many happy hours playing with her six daughters – one of whom eventually married Tutankhamun – in the palace of Akhet-Aten.

The Holy City

Constructed in record time and abandoned equally rapidly on the death of its founder, Akhet-Aten originally stretched for eight miles along the Nile.

At its centre lay a complex of palaces and temples, all of them revolving around the enormous Temple of the Sun's Disk.

Life and leisure

Formal and stylised as most Egyptian art was – with the exception of the Amarna style – it has many little human and individual touches that bring to life the day-to-day activities of the people. Tomb paintings show vivid scenes of hunting in the deserts and marshes, of feasts and parties, games and dancing: all the activities that wealthy Egyptians hoped to continue in the next world.

Only the upper classes – nobles, distinguished soldiers and administrators – lived as well as this. Their large estates were overseen for them by scribes, who kept a careful record for their masters of all the crops grown and harvested and numbers of animals reared. Hosts of servants toiled in the vineyards, picking grapes and treading them for wine. They looked after the herds of cattle, goat and antelope, too, which provided meat for the table.

Whole families spent the day hunting on the banks of the Nile with boomerangs. This seems to have been one of the favourite sports of the Ancient Egyptians. A famous fresco shows a man killing wildfowl in the marshes, with his wife and children – and pet cat!

The family could relax in the garden of their villa, sitting round a pool enjoying the scent of flowers. Girls played with dolls or practised dancing. When boys were not studying, they wrestled or played tug-of-war. Adults could amuse themselves with board games similar to chess or drafts.

Rich households had large numbers of indoor servants to cook, brew beer, launder, weave linen for clothes and serve at table. They must have worked hard during feasts – which seem to have been very popular. Long tables groaned under dishes of meat, game, fruit, bread and pastries. Guests drank huge quantities of wine and beer – the Egyptians enjoyed drinking, and its effects!

Men and women both wore eye paint and ladies fixed cones of incense on their heads so that, as the party wore on, the melting grease perfumed their hair. Guests were entertained by singers and dancing girls to the music of harps and flutes, and dwarves and acrobats performed tricks.

A nobleman's estate

Surrounded by high walls and formal gardens, a rich family's country residence was like a well-ordered village. Kitchens, workshops, servants' quarters, storerooms, grain silos and sheds for animals stood apart from the central mansion. Near the entrance was a chapel. In the spacious mud-brick house, a large living area, its ceiling supported by columns, led to the master bedroom, bathrooms and lavatories at the rear. Stairs gave access to the roof.

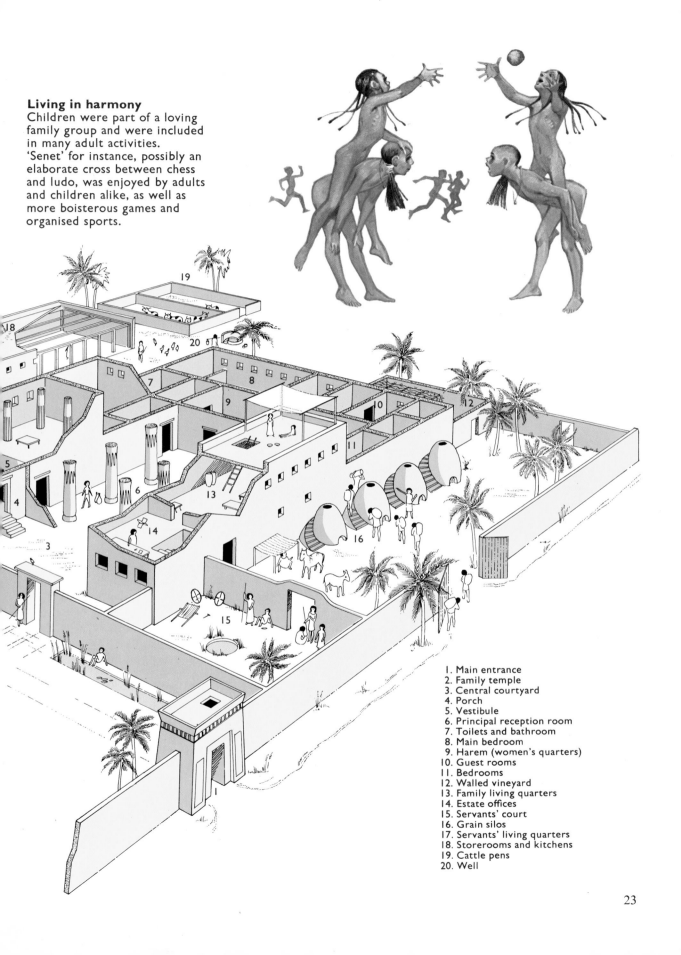

Living in harmony

Children were part of a loving family group and were included in many adult activities. 'Senet' for instance, possibly an elaborate cross between chess and ludo, was enjoyed by adults and children alike, as well as more boisterous games and organised sports.

1. Main entrance
2. Family temple
3. Central courtyard
4. Porch
5. Vestibule
6. Principal reception room
7. Toilets and bathroom
8. Main bedroom
9. Harem (women's quarters)
10. Guest rooms
11. Bedrooms
12. Walled vineyard
13. Family living quarters
14. Estate offices
15. Servants' court
16. Grain silos
17. Servants' living quarters
18. Storerooms and kitchens
19. Cattle pens
20. Well

Education and ambition

Schools for scribes

A New Kingdom scribe studied for about 12 years to learn the 700-odd hieroglyphs in use at the time. Five-year-old boys spent endless hours copying individual signs as well as whole passages from textbooks. Older pupils learned letter-writing, book-keeping, mathematics and astronomy – the subjects they might need in their careers.

Painted wooden statue of a New Kingdom scribe circa 1500 BC

The beginner's materials

Only fully-qualified scribes wrote on the beautiful paper made from papyrus. Students practised their hieroglyphs on potsherds (flakes of pottery or stone) or on wooden tablets. They wrote with reed pens or with brushes dipped in water and lampblack.

In the complex society of Ancient Egypt, the scribe was as important as the office worker is today in our own community. His work was similar too – writing letters, making reports, recording events and keeping accounts of produce – but his social position was much more important. He could rise to really high office because of his ability to read and write.

At school, Egyptian boys were taught reading and writing and arithmetic to fit them for careers in government service, as priests or as administrators for wealthy men. Good handwriting and com-position were both learnt by copying models. A scribe had to know the different styles used for different sorts of letters. A petition written for an illiterate person to a great man, for instance, would have to be put in very flowery language to please the influential reader.

At first a scribe might be employed in calculating areas of land or the numbers of blocks of stone quarried for a pyramid, record-ing tax payments or the distribution of rations to the army. He might work for a wealthy family, for the army, or among govern-ment officials and priests. But if he were ambitious, he could rise through the ranks of the army or the civil service to hold a power-

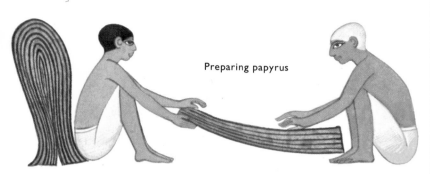

Preparing papyrus

The Rosetta Stone

The slab of basalt, found near Rosetta in 1799, showed three scripts – hieroglyphic (A), demotic (B) and Greek (C). Groups of ringed hieroglyphs

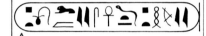

A

(cartouches) were found to tally with the Greek names of rulers. Champollion identified the symbols and their sounds (p, o, l) common to the names

B

of Ptolemy and Cleopatra and worked out the remaining letters by their positions. At last the words on the Rosetta Stone could be read.

ΠΤΟΛΕΜΑΙΟΣ

C

ful office, such as chief of public works, royal architect, or even governor of one of Egypt's provinces, called nomes.

The professional scribe recorded all his information on clay tablets or papyrus scrolls. Paper was made by cutting thin strips of pith, the spongy tissue in the stem of a papyrus reed, and arranging them crosswise on a flat stone. The papyrus was then beaten with wooden mallets until the natural juice, acting like glue, bound the strips together. Then the single sheets were pasted into one long roll.

The Egyptians had perfected the technique of paper-making as early as the Ist dynasty and their written language dates from this time. Hieroglyphs, or miniature pictures, sometimes represent a whole word or idea and are called ideograms. Thus the word for house ⬜ looks like a simple diagram of a house. Other hieroglyphs have a phonetic, or sound, value and are called phonograms. The owl, 🦉 for instance, indicates the sound 'm' and a snake ～ the sound 'f'. There were hundreds of such signs and they could be written in whatever form was most pleasing to the scribe: from left to right, from right to left, or vertically in columns.

Although hieroglyphic writing continued to be used for sacred inscriptions in tombs and temples, a less elaborate system called hieratic, was evolved for everyday use. Simple strokes replaced the complex symbols and made this form of writing more convenient. Much later, in about 700 BC, writing was further developed into so-called demotic script.

By the 4th century AD the meaning of the ancient hieroglyphs had been lost. It was not until 1822 that Jean François Champollion, a young French linguist, deciphered the hieroglyphs on the Rosetta Stone and opened up the secrets of a great civilisation.

Scribes at work

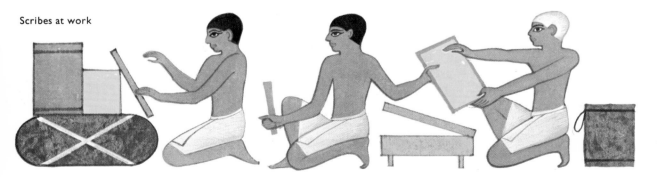

Preparation for immortality

An Ancient Egyptian thought that the land of the dead would be very much like the Nile valley. He believed that when he died he would travel there and live in eternal happiness with the gods. At first, only royalty was thought to enjoy an after-life, but, by the time of the New Kingdom, nobles, and eventually commoners, believed that they would live for ever.

If the dead man's *ka*, or spirit, was to survive, his body had to be preserved. The embalmer first removed the brain, then all the contents of the stomach and chest except the heart. The heart was thought to be the seat of intelligence and would be needed for judgement in the underworld. The empty body was then washed with palm wine and spices and covered with sodium salts for 70 days to dry it out. The intestines and other vital organs were mummified and put in four containers called the Canopic Jars. The dried body was packed with linen and spices, rubbed with oils

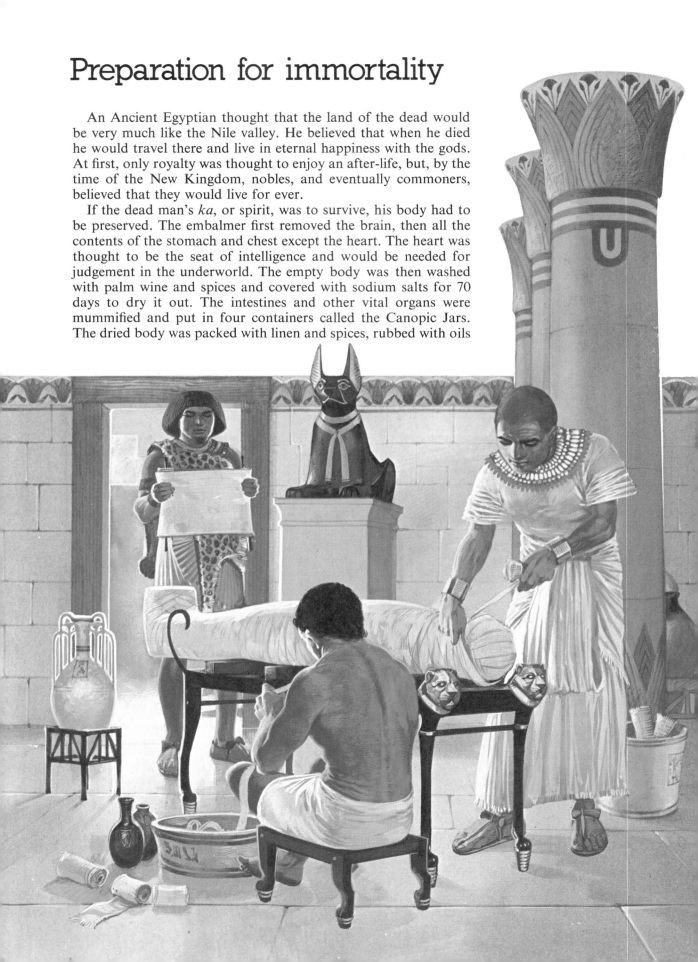

or wine and coated with melted resin. As the bandaging began, prayers were recited from the *Book of the Dead*. Sometimes sacred amulets (charms against evil) like the *ankh*, symbol of life, were swathed in the linen. Finally, encased in its coffin, the mummy was borne in procession from the east bank of the Nile, where priests and family performed ceremonies which would restore the dead man to life.

Because the next world reflected, as in a mirror, the present one, the dead person was buried with furniture, hunting equipment, clothes, jewellery and models of his servants. Food for his *ka* was to be left daily in an adjoining shrine. The *ka* could only survive if it had nourishment (which could be ensured by reciting the right prayers too) and a habitation – the tomb. The desecrations of the tomb robbers were regarded with horror because they destroyed the occupants' hopes of eternal life.

Animals honoured in death
Beasts associated with the gods were frequently mummified. The scarab beetle, crocodile and cat were all embalmed and buried either with humans or in their own sacred cemeteries.

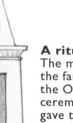

A ritual farewell
The mummy is supported as the family and priests perform the Opening of the Mouth ceremony. They believed this gave the dead man the power to breathe.

Travel in the next world
Model boats similar to those which bore the dead pharaohs across the Nile, were often entombed. This one is carved with the head of Hathor.

Judgement among the gods
A feather, symbol of *maet*, or truth, is weighed against the dead man's heart. Several gods look on as the balance is presented to the supreme judge, Osiris for his verdict.

27

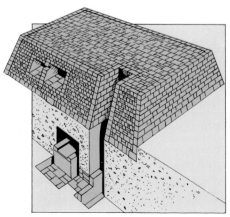

The mastabas
These were rectangular structures of unbaked mud-brick. Architectural versions of prehistoric burial mounds, they grew large enough to house stores as well as bodies.

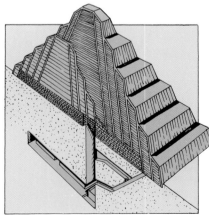

The step pyramid at Saqqara
The world's oldest stone building, raised by the architect Imhotep for King Zoser, consists of a million tonnes of solid rock. Imhotep became so famous that he was later worshipped as a god.

The Mountains of Pharaoh

There are about 80 pyramids, dotted along the edge of the Nile. The Arabs called them 'the Mountains of Pharaoh'. To the Egyptians, the pyramids were vast tombs, built to ensure a glorious afterlife for their rulers.

Until the IIIrd dynasty all Egyptian buildings were of mud-brick. Then King Zoser built a step pyramid of stone instead of the usual *mastaba*, the subterranean, earth-covered tomb of his ancestors. A century after Zoser another ruler, Cheops, raised the most massive of the true pyramids, the Great Pyramid of Giza.

At Giza, gangs of labourers, using copper chisels and saws, cut the stones from nearby cliff quarries, then levered them on to sledges and hauled them with palm-fibre ropes to the site. The 15-tonne granite blocks were floated down the Nile on barges from Aswan, 800 kilometres away. Skilled masons laid a central core of solid masonry and chambers and passages were tunnelled deep into the heart of it. As the pyramid rose, trimmed blocks were dragged up great ramps of earth and rubble and levered into position on a skin of liquid mortar. The valley building, where the pharaoh's funeral procession would eventually disembark, was constructed by the river and a covered causeway was laid from it to the ceremonial mortuary temple. Finally, the pyramid itself was faced with polished limestone or granite and the galleries inside were carved and painted with scenes from the pharaoh's life. Cheops' son, Chephron, and his grandson, Mycerinus, built their own pyramids at the same site.

Guardian of the dead
The Great Sphinx, crouched in the sand at Giza, has defended the pyramids for 46 centuries.

Rediscovery

The obscure immortal
Almost 1000 years before
Tutankhamun was buried in the
Valley of the Kings at Thebes, all
the great pyramids had already
been entered and robbed. Most
of the tombs at Thebes suffered
the same fate. Only Tutankhamun's has been found intact
and for this reason it is one of
the most exciting archaeological
discoveries in history. The young
pharaoh was entombed with an
astonishing array of golden
animals, statues, alabaster vases,
magnificent furniture and
weapons. In one chamber the
mummified body of Tutan-
khamun, undisturbed for 3000-
odd years, lay in a coffin of solid
gold. Placed over his head was
the golden portrait mask
illustrated above. The beaten
gold has been inlaid with blue
glass and encrusted with lapis
lazuli, a semi-precious stone. The
vulture and cobra on the king's
headdress, have also been
fashioned from gold. Yet Tutankhamun was an obscure king who
died when about eighteen and
only ruled for nine years. The
wealth of the really powerful
New Kingdom pharaohs must
have been truly incredible.

The civilisation of Ancient Egypt died 2000 years ago, but along
the banks of the Nile its people left a timeless record of their
lives, their religion and their achievements. Almost at the dawn of
history the Egyptians were writing hieroglyphs and painting scenes
on the walls of their temples and tombs. Many of the monuments
they built had in antiquity been plundered for stone by other
builders, destroyed by jealous pharaohs, or robbed of their trea-
sures by thieves. Yet a remarkably consistent picture of the Egyptian way of life has been unravelled from what evidence survives
by scholars who have painstakingly excavated buildings, examined
mummies and pored over the inscriptions on the walls and in the
beautiful papyrus scrolls.

True scientific research in Egypt dates from 1799 when linguists
began the struggle to decipher the hieroglyphs on the Rosetta
Stone. By 1822, as the Egyptian language started to yield its
secrets, a wave of interest in the ancient land swept over Europe.
In the late 19th century there was increased excitement when two
great caches of mummies were discovered at Thebes. Among the
33 royal coffins were those of Ahmose I, the founder of the New
Kingdom, Tuthmosis III and Ramesses II. Centuries ago priests
had removed all these mummies from their original tombs and re-
buried them in secret chambers as a protection against tomb
robbers. X-ray examination of the bodies has revealed details about
the diet of the Ancient Egyptians, their lifespan, their diseases and
medical treatments and the techniques of embalming.

The dry, desert air of Egypt has preserved almost everything –
from the mummies themselves to rope, papyrus, cloth, gold and
even wood. In 1954, the wooden funerary boat, over 40 metres
long, which bore the body of Cheops across the Nile to Giza, was
unearthed near his Great Pyramid. Made of cedar from the
Lebanon, the boat is in almost perfect condition. Twelve years
later two bodies were found at Saqqara in the tomb of an Old
Kingdom court official called Nefer. These bodies, and their
vividly decorated burial chamber, had been preserved for 4500
years.

In Nubia, the Egyptianised land to the south of Aswan, more
than twenty historic monuments have been rescued from the lake
created by the building of the Aswan High Dam. At Abu Simbel,
the temple of Ramesses II and that of his queen, Nefertari, were
cut into 30-tonne blocks and removed to an identical site above the
level of the new lake. Cutting and lifting the huge stones required
as much engineering skill as the original builders displayed when
they erected the vast temples. But, inevitably in a land so rich in
ancient remains, much of Nubia has become a drowned museum
of temples, towns and fortresses.

Probably no project or discovery in Egypt has captured the
imagination so much as the opening of Tutankhamun's tomb in
1922. Yet, more than 50 years later, archaeologists are still making
startling discoveries and the desert sands of Egypt may hold even
more undreamed of secrets.

Index